Alright!
The story of Queen at
Live Aid

Glen Humphries

Last Day of School
Lastdayofschool.net

ISBN: 978-0-6489911-0-6

ABOUT THE AUTHOR

Glen Humphries is a multi award-winning journalist and author. Since 2017 he's been writing and publishing books under his own imprint, Last Day of School. In that time he has largely written books about beer, music and footy – with a diversion to a true crime book about a serial criminal in the area he grew up in. This is his 10th book – which comes as a surprise to him. After all, he only figured he had one book in him. He acknowledges that it would have made far more sense to have had this book out when the movie *Bohemian Rhapsody* was released and everyone was going nuts for Queen. But he missed that boat – big time. He is oddly impressed that Brian May found a hairstyle that worked for him back in the early 1970s and stuck with it for more than five decades. He still can't believe the director of *Flash Gordon* thought he was making a serious movie. The guy was there on-set, how could he not see how camp and jokey it was? To be honest, that jokey character is the reason it's a cult classic – if it was serious, then it would have been quite dull. By the way, Glen still listens to the *Flash Gordon* soundtrack and will buy it on vinyl if he ever finds it. He wonders if anyone still listens to the *Hot Space* album. *Hammer to Fall* is his favourite song from the Live Aid set.

Also by Glen Humphries and published by Last Day of School (www.lastdayofschool.net)

The Slab: 24 Stories of Beer in Australia
James Squire: The Biography
The Six-Pack: Stories from the World of Beer
Friday Night at the Oxford
Beer Is Fun
Sounds Like an Ending: Midnight Oil, 10-1 and Red Sails in the Sunset
Night Terrors: The True Story of the Kingsgrove Slasher
Biff: Rugby League's Infamous Fights
Healer: The Rise, Fall and Return of Tumbleweed

6.41pm
Bohemian Rhapsody

They take to the stage early on a summer's evening to the roar of the crowd that sounds like a single beast rather than a collection of thousands of voices. The roar could well be because they figure anyone will be more exciting than the snore-inducing Dire Straits who had left the stage not too long ago, after inflicting upon the audience an 11-minute version of *Sultans of Swing*.

There are four of them who take the stage, two run to the far side - one with an exaggerated stride. The other two are only spied in the wide shot, bowing to the crowd before moving to their respective spots on the stage.

There are four of them, but the camera has already worked out who the star is; the one with that exaggerated stride, the one who shadow boxes with the crowd. The one wearing the runners, tight jeans and equally tight singlet – all of which he had been wearing as he made his way to the gig.

Like everyone else, the camera has figured out Freddie Mercury is the star of the show, the magnet for your attention. And it's still the case on the Live Aid stage, even though John Deacon's impressive afro deserves far more camera time than he gets. Mercury walks back across the stage, waving to the masses with a big grin before taking a seat at the piano located at the front of the stage. He plays a few recognisable notes – well, they're recognisable if you know what's coming – before tweaking a knob to improve the sound. Then his fingers start the song, the left hand crossing over to the high notes, which is the moment the crowd squeals (yes, that's the word for it), because the penny has dropped. They know the song – and they know the words.

This is where Queen's show starts. But it's not where the story begins; for that we have to go back eight months. Which seems such a short amount of time to allow for these things to happen…

It's the night of October 24, 1984, in a home in Chelsea, a district not all that far from the home of the British PM. There sitting in that Chelsea home is a man by the name of Bob Geldof. Sure, the name is immediately recognisable now. These days everyone has heard of Sir Bob. But it wasn't the case back in 1984. Back then he was a fading rock star, the frontman of The Boomtown Rats, who hadn't had a top 10 hit in the UK for the last two years. Their latest album had been released in May that year and hadn't set the charts on fire. Had the events over the coming eight months never happened, he'd be best known for singing *I Don't Like Mondays*, the song FM radio DJs love to play at the start of the working week.

That night, Geldof sits down with his girlfriend Paula Yates and switches on the TV to the BBC to watch *The Six O'Clock News*. That night he sees a seven-minute news story that puts his struggle to get radio to play the Rats new single into perspective, a story that shocks him. A story that changes the trajectory of his life.

"In Ethiopia seven million people are threatened by starvation," said BBC newsreader Julia Somerville. "Thousands have already died. The famine, caused by drought, is the worst in living memory and now the rains have failed again for the third year in succession."

A secessionist war in the north of the country has made the situation worse, forcing 40,000 refugees inland to the town of Korem looking for food and medical help. The BBC's Michael Buerk was in that town and filed a harrowing news story.

The camera pans over a massive crowd of people sitting on the bare ground, shrouded in thin blankets – a crowd that spreads as far into the distance as the eye can see. "Dawn, and as the sun breaks through the piercing chill of night on the plain outside Korem," Buerk said in his introduction, "it lights up a biblical famine, now, in the 20th century. This place, say workers here, is the closest thing to hell on earth."

"It did not look like television," Geldof would remember. "Vast ... grey ... these grey wraiths moving about this moonscape."

Buerk would keep talking throughout the report, but the images alone told the horrible story. There are the desperate, keening cries of hungry, confused children. A man walks into the frame carrying what at first glance appears to be a bundle of sticks - and then you realise it's the lifeless body of his child wrapped in blankets. A crowd of children rush to a truck because of a rumour it is carrying food (it isn't); the crowd includes one boy teetering along on impossibly thin legs while struggling under the weight of the younger sibling he carries in his arms.

Aid workers have the horrible task of picking which refugees will get wheat. Those who miss out will bend over and pick up any stray grains of wheat that have fallen to the ground, collecting them in a blanket. A woman lacks the energy to wave away the flies that crawl over her face. The body of another woman is wrapped in cloth and bound with rope, her feet sticking out the bottom. Between her own feet

5

are two more tiny feet – those of her two-month-old baby who died with her.

Buerk would interview a doctor from Medecins Sans Frontieres, who expected hundreds of thousands would die in Korem if nothing was done to help.

"It was clear that was a tragedy which the world had somehow contrived not to notice until it had reached a scale which constituted an international scandal," Geldof said. "You could hear that in the tones of the reporter. It was not the usual dispassionate objectivity of the BBC. It was the voice of a man who was registering despair, grief and absolute disgust at what he was seeing."

He spent that night wondering what he could do to help. He thought first of sending some money, but figured it would be a tiny drop in a very, very big – and largely empty – bucket. Next he figured the Boomtown Rats could help - he'd donate the profits of their next record to Oxfam, as small as those profits may be.

"It would be a pitiful amount," he said. "But it would be more than I could raise by simply dipping into my shrunken bank account."

The following day, the idea of some sort of charity record had firmed in Geldof's mind. He headed into the offices of the Rats' record label to continue with the promotion of their next single, which now seemed meaningless compared to what he'd seen the night before.

Back in the 1980s, TV was very different. There was no streaming, no plethora of digital channels, no downloading shows. You watched a show when a channel decided to air it. That meant there was a whole lot of eyeballs on each show. Which was the case with that episode of the *Nine O'Clock News*. Buerk estimated the show had a nightly audience of 10 million.

Among those 10 million was everyone in the record label press office that morning. They had all seen these horrifying footage of emaciated children and desperate parents, so when Geldof told them of his ideas for a charity single, they all offered encouragement.

But there was still the problem that the Boomtown Rats just wouldn't sell that many records. Maybe he could ask some other people to join in ...

Really, it was a no-brainer than Queen would play *Bohemian Rhapsody* at some stage in their 17-odd minutes at Wembley. But just how much of it could they get away with? On the *Night at the Opera* album it clocks in at 5.53 - play the whole thing at Live Aid and it chews up one-third of their stage time. Then of course there's the issue that they actually can't play the whole thing live; in their own concerts when the "Gallileos" come in, they just walk off stage for just over a minute while a recording of the operatic bit plays. Then they sneak back on in darkness, and the stage lights explode when the hard rock "spit in my eye" bit starts.

Admittedly they can get away with it at their own shows, it even adds to the drama. But at Live Aid they're playing in daylight; no-one can turn off the stage lights to shield the stars' temporarily absence. The 72,000 at Wembley and the almost 2 billion watching at home would see them slink off and be forced to stare at an empty stage for a minute.

So they cut it in half – and then some. At Live Aid the song goes for nigh on two minutes - one-third of the full run time. By today's standards, a five-minute, 53 second song isn't really *that* unusual, but back in the mid-1970s it was long enough to give record company bosses heart palpitations. In a time when radio airplay was everything when it came to record sales, any song pushing three minutes and change was commercial poison. The stations just wouldn't play it. If it had an operatic section, well, kiss any chance of airplay goodbye.

Mercury hadn't decided to write such a long song on a whim; the idea had been kicking around longer than Queen had existed. He had the "momma, just killed a man" bit about five years earlier, and thought of it as "the cowboy song". By early 1975 he had the pieces together, at least in his head. *A Night at the Opera* producer Roy Thomas Baker remembers Mercury playing the tune to him before they went out for dinner. He played the first section on the piano, leading Baker to conclude it was a ballad. "He played a bit further through the song and then stopped suddenly, saying 'this is where the opera section comes in'. We both burst out laughing."

But Mercury wasn't kidding. Baker would find that out during the recording sessions when the band laid down the beginning and the end with the producer leaving blank tape in the middle for the opera section.

Soon enough the Gallileos, Bizmillahs and Beelzebubs kept coming, so many that the repeated recordings led to that section showing real signs of wear. "The original tape had actually worn thin," May remembered. "People think it's this legendary story, but you could hold the tape up to the light and see through it. Every time the tape went through the heads, more of the oxide was worn off." Every 'Gallileo' that went on meant something else was lost.

The band backed Mercury's call to release *Bohemian Rhapsody* as the first single, a month ahead of *A Night at the Opera* hitting the shops (though for some reason *The Prophet's Song* was also in the mix at one stage). And the record company had it wrong; radio stations *did* play it. People went and bought it too; pushing it to No1 on the UK charts for more than two months.

The song also popularised the idea of bands making music videos for their latest single. For Queen, a video for *Bohemian Rhapsody* made sense; they were never going to be able to perform the whole thing live on a TV show. In part influenced by the cover of album *Queen II*, the video only took a few hours. Director Bruce Gowers said they started filming at 7pm one night and were in the pub before it closed at 11pm. He also admitted some of the special effects were decidedly low-tech. "That famous multiplying effect during the 'thunderbolts and lightning' part, where you see many Freddie Mercurys and Brian Mays? That was corny. I stuck a prism onto the camera lens. It was held on with gaffer tape."

The meaning behind the song has always been a mystery, with Mercury playing his cards close to his chest. "People should just listen to it, think about it and then decide what it means". May also figured it was better people took away their own meanings. "I don't think we'll ever know and if I knew I probably wouldn't want to tell you anyway. But the great thing about a great song is that you relate it to your own personal experiences in your own life." That's part of the appeal of not knowing the story behind the song - you can come up with your own.

People might want the band to spill the beans but if they did that then the mystery would be over. And maybe some people would feel the real story actually wrecked their preferred version. Taylor couldn't understand what all the bother was about; "It's fairly self-explanatory - there's just a bit of nonsense in the middle.

It would be Taylor who would end up the surprising winner from *Bohemian Rhapsody*'s success. For it was he who had the song on the B-side – *I'm in Love with My Car*. The story goes that Taylor locked himself in a closet until the band agreed his song would occupy the flip side. That meant every time someone bought a copy of "Bo Rap", his song registered a sale as well (though it's hard to imagine anyone picked up the single because of the B-side – the song is a little bit crap).

"A lot of terrible injustices take place over songwriting," May said. "The major one is B-sides. *Bohemian Rhapsody* sells a million and Roger gets the same writing royalties as Freddie because he did *I'm in Love with My Car*. There was contention about that for years." But they'd finally fix up the royalty situation - which was a good thing too as money tends to be the source of many a band break-up.

6.43pm
Radio Gaga

So Geldof has decided a charity single – one performed by people more popular than his band – is the way to go. Which leaves him short an actual song. Not long after his brainwave, Geldof arranged to go out to lunch with Midge Ure, a friend of his and Paula's. The lead singer and songwriter with Ultravox,

Ure was having all the chart success Geldof wasn't – in the first half of the '80s, they'd had 17 singles in the UK top 40 (their highest placing was #2 in 1981 with *Vienna*). Ure realised later he got the call because the hit-free Geldof lacked the confidence to ring up some heavy hitter like Sting and ask him to write the song.

With Geldof figuring the record had to be out quickly so as to capitalise on the Christmas rush, they first talked about recording a cover version, but that was scratched out because half of the money raised would go to the songwriter. So, given they were both songwriters (one perhaps a tad more successful than the other) they decided to come up with something themselves.

"We realised that what we had to do was write and record a new song and we only had a few weeks left before Christmas," Ure said.

Geldof admitted he had a bit of a song that had been kicking around called *It's My World*, and Ure said he'd go away, have a think and try to come up with something.

Meanwhile, Geldof also hit the phones to try to come up with some famous voices to sing this song that hadn't been written. Sting was up for it, so were

Duran Duran as long as it didn't clash with their upcoming German tour. He spotted Gary Kemp from Spandau Ballet in an antique store and got that band signed up. He added Boy George and Jon Moss from Culture Club, Paul Young and Paul Weller to the list. Suddenly he realised they had enough people to make this thing work.

But they still needed that song. In the back of a taxi on the way to a friend's house, Geldof dashed out the words in his diary. "I wrote fluently, with little crossing out. The words poured out. I wanted to evoke pity and concern and I wanted to make people think."

Geldof's song had the line "there won't be snow in Ethiopia this Christmas-time" but Ure felt it didn't track well and suggested changing it to "Africa". That would later draw criticism, because it does in fact snow in some parts of Africa.

For his bit, Ure had sat down with his little Casio keyboard and thought 'Christmas'. "I came up with this bell sound," Ure said, "a little third harmony part that made it sound familiar and added a touch of *Jingle Bells*."

Geldof's bit was the first two verses of the song

and Ure had come up with the melody (and that drum sound at the start, which he sampled from Tears for Fears' *The Hurting* single) that is really the reason it gets played every Christmas time. But they still didn't have a full song.

After discussing it for a while, they realised raising a glass in a toast is something people did at Christmas, and so that became the basis of the middle eight that kicks in after the verses.

Then one of them – Ure said he doesn't remember who it was – came up with the 'Do they know it's Christmas' line which immediately became the hook line in the song (that title would later cause friction because around 40 per cent of Africa's population is Christian, so *of course* they'd know it's Christmas-time). It was Geldof who recognised the song needed to end on a singalong anthem, much like *Give Peace a Chance*.

On top of getting the song sorted and lining up the musicians, Geldof had a load of other headaches to deal with. He had meetings with Phonogram bosses to find out what needed to be done, he got artist Peter Blake (responsible for The Beatles' *Sgt Pepper's Lonely Hearts Club Band* cover) to put together something for *Do They Know It's Christmas* in a hurry.

He spoke to Wham's manager Simon Napier Bell about getting George and Andrew on board. The manager also gave Geldof a primer on how many people take their cut from record sales and how he'd have to get them to forego that to raise enough money.

The Rats' frontman had to convince record store retailers to donate their cut, which he did by telling each of them all the others had already agreed – they hadn't. Under a Musicians Union deal, every time the BBC played the song, a fee had to be paid to the artists – and with almost 40 performers, it would cost the Beeb a fortune. So they most likely wouldn't have played it all. Geldof had gone so far as to look to create a rival union to make its own agreement with the BBC, but the Musicians Union was quite happy to support the cause.

Phonogram was willing to waive their profit. The big problem was the Thatcher government which would refuse to waive the tax it would collect on the record sales. Though, curiously, it would make a donation to the cause of *exactly* the same amount as the tax raised.

On Sunday, November 25 the members of Band

Aid (rejected names included 'Food for Thought' and 'The Bloody Do-Gooders') turned up at the studio, where the press was waiting to snap pictures of the stars' arrival. Some – like Spandau Ballet – got it wrong by rolling up in limousines. Not a good look when you're recording a single for starving people.

"Everyone knows how to be humble now, but not then," says Spandau's Gary Kemp. "Sting got it perfectly right. He walked up the road with a copy of the *Guardian* under his arm. He probably got his driver to drop him off round the corner, but it looked as though he was completely on-message. He knew what to do immediately."

There were some surprises among the arrivals; US band Kool and the Gang were in the country and got in on the action. UK singer Marilyn hadn't been invited by anyone but turned up anyway. Comedian Nigel Planer, who played Neil in *The Young Ones* and had a hit that year with *There's a Hole in My Shoe*, gate-crashed the event in character and was tolerated for a while before being shown the door.

To get everyone warmed up, Ure started at the end – with the massed choir singing the 'Feed the World' part. Ure double-tracked this part to make it sound like there was even more people there.

When it came to singing individual lines, Ure and Geldof hadn't worked out who would get which line. So each performer sang several lines and Ure would later edit it to suit. After much reluctance from all the singers, Spandau Ballet's Tony Hadley was the first to step up to the mike for his solo lines. "Nobody likes singing in the studio," Geldof wrote in his autobiography. "You do it with the backing track being played to you though the headphones. All anybody else in the studio can hear is your weedy strainings. It usually sounds awful and at that moment there were still four different TV crews in there filming." Not to mention just about all their musical contemporaries standing and watching them.

Bono from U2 would end up with one of the more uncomfortable lines, the one about thanking God it's them instead of you. For many it sounds a bit callous, as though there's some glee in avoiding that suffering.

Bono certainly wasn't comfortable singing it, according to Ure. "He was not scared to query Bob. 'Why,' he said, 'would I want somebody else to go through this?'

"Bob was a real stickler for his words and what

they meant and he had a very different angle on what the line meant. He told Bono, 'I'm not saying I want somebody else to suffer, I'm saying I'm glad it's not you'."

Putting so many musicians together in one place and it's highly likely that a few tensions might erupt. The oft-grumpy Paul Weller decided to have a go at George Michael who silenced him with the killer line, "don't be a wanker all your life. Have a day off".

Other musicians forget they were there to help raise money for victims of famine. "At some point somebody asked, 'hey Bob, where's the food?'" Band Aid video director Nigel Dick said. "And he completely lost it. He said 'This is a fucking charity record and people are starving. Go buy your own fucking lunch."

And of course, there were drugs. It's a roomful of musicians, how could there not be drugs? For that you can blame Francis Rossi and Rick Parfitt from Status Quo. That band seemed a bit out of their element among all the Spandaus, Durans, Whams and Culture Clubs. But Geldof had wanted them because it meant their large fan base would buy the single. The other bands were happy they were there because they brought a big bag of coke – and were happy to share it. "Everybody was just totally out of it and Rick and I were the drug centre," Rossi said. "People were saying, 'let's go and see Dr Rossi and Dr Parfitt, shall we?" It was crazy, a really crazy day. There were shitloads of drugs – coke, dope, all sorts."

Two people unlikely to be partaking were Geldof and Ure, who were still working on the recording at 6pm. That's when Boy George finally arrived, having woken up that morning in New York by an angry Geldof on the phone and told to get his arse on the next Concorde.

The bleary-eyed pair wrapped up the mixing at 7am the following day. Geldof took a copy to the BBC and told them to "play it all the time". Introducing the first playing of the song, Geldof told the listeners all the cash was going to Ethiopia.

"Even if you've never bought a record in your life before, get it," he said. "It's only £1.30. That's how cheap it is to give someone the ultimate Christmas gift – their life. It's pathetic but the price of a life this year is a piece of plastic with a hole in the middle."

It worked. Within a week, advance orders reached 250,000. The single was released on December 3. By

December 9 orders had reached the one million mark – Phonogram had to put five of its European plants to work pressing the single.

"People were buying boxes of the record and sending them out as Christmas cards," Geldof said. "Others walked in, bought 50, kept one, and then gave the other 49 back for resale. A butcher in Plymouth rang me to ask if you needed special permission to sell records. When I said no, he got rid of all the meat from his window and filled it with the record. The Queen's grocer, Fortnum and Mason, phoned to ask for two boxes to sell in their restaurant; by the end they had sold thousands there."

The week before the single was released Jim Diamond had the No1 spot on the charts with *I Should Have Known Better*. "I'm delighted to be No1," he said, "but next week I don't want people to buy my record, I want them to buy Band Aid instead." It was a noble gesture, but one that didn't offer immediate benefits for Band Aid. The following week Frankie Goes to Hollywood would sneak into the top spot with *The Power of Love*. *Do They Know it's Christmas* would hit No1 a week later and would stay there until the second week of January 1985. And it would make more than £8 million.

Not bad for something Geldof thought would sell just 72,000 copies.

Queen didn't appear on the Band Aid song, much to Mercury's later disappointment, "We would have liked to have taken part in the Band Aid single," he said, 'but I think we were in separate parts of the globe."

In their autobiographies neither Geldof nor Ure makes any mention of Queen even being considered for Band Aid. That oversight wouldn't have been due to any concerns over their pulling power. The band's latest album, *The Works*, had been released in February 1984 and would reach No2 on the UK charts. The first single, *Radio Ga Ga* would also be a hit and make it to the second spot on the charts. Second single *I Want to Break Free* would reach No3. *It's a Hard Life* would hit No6 and the fourth single *Hammer to Fall*, released just a month before Buerk's Ethiopia report would air, stopped just outside the top 10.

So there's no question of them being a band past

their prime or old and out of touch – if they were Geldof wouldn't have pursued them for Live Aid just six month later. The most likely reason Queen wasn't asked to appear on the Christmas 1984 single was due to their horrible decision to play in South Africa a few months earlier during the apartheid regime – in contravention of a United Nations boycott. The band played a long run of shows at Sun City, a casino-and-golf resort for the rich, the last one just days before Geldof had the idea for Band Aid. Queen's decision would be widely and justly criticised in the UK and the band would be fined by the Musicians Union.

It was a staggeringly naïve decision from the band; they seemed unable to grasp that playing Sun City signaled a tacit approval of apartheid – regardless of the band's intentions (though manager Jim Beach said the principal reason they went was because they got paid wads of cash).

The band's later comments did them no favours. "We've thought a lot about the morals of it and it is something we've decided to do," May said at the time. "The band is not political – we play to anybody who wants to come and listen."

John Deacon didn't help by saying "I know there

can be a bit of a fuss but apparently we're very popular down there."

Years later Roger Taylor got it when he said "on balance, I think it was a mistake to go".

There would be little doubt the South African tour was why Queen were overlooked for Band Aid. Yes, the members might have been scattered all over the globe but that hardly matters, given they weren't asked to play in the first place.

Obviously by July 1985 they had served their time in purgatory and were asked to join Live Aid. There would be one other Sun City alumni on the bill – Elton John had played there almost a year earlier than Queen. Also, Live Aid opener Status Quo would take the cash and play there in October 1987.

The band didn't take part in the biggest Christmas single of the year, but Queen did release their own festive tune. *Thank God it's Christmas* made the charts but it didn't perform anywhere near as well as the Band Aid tune, reaching no higher than No21 on the UK charts.

That song didn't make the Live Aid setlist, but three songs released that year would – the first of them would be the second song, *Radio Ga Ga*, the band moving straight into it from the abbreviated *Bohemian Rhapsody*. Mercury stands up from the piano, legs in a wide stance and puts a celebratory fist in the air before reaching for his sawn-off microphone stand.

It's not immediately apparent what the next song; the band is playing a crescendo of sorts in an effort to get from one tune to the next. But by the time Mercury reaches centre stage the keyboard and drumbeat of *Radio Ga Ga* kicks in.

The crowd roars; they know this one. It had been released six months earlier and went all the way to No2, held off by Frankie Goes to Hollywood's *Relax*. The crowd is into it and so is Mercury; strutting across the stage, playing up to the masses at Wembley even before the lyrics begin. The cameras know it too; there isn't a single shot in the whole song that doesn't include Mercury.

The highlight for many happens in the choruses, as the fans copy the raised arm actions from the video. It doesn't happen immediately; despite Mercury urging them to join in, a shot of him from behind shows the crowd a bit cautious, a bit pensive. It's not really until the fourth cycle that they get into it.

There are two different crowd actions from the video; one where they raise their arms and then clap twice with the beat and a second where the fists are just held out for a few seconds. The audience wisely chose to perform the first; it's more instinctive and it just looks better. The band were surprised to see the crowd unite as one. Used to playing at night with the crowd in darkness, they'd had little idea what was going on out there. But just before 7pm, the sun was still up at Wembley and Queen was showing the world they could perform without the expensive light show and smoke machines.

"I remember Freddie being stunned when he launched into *Radio Ga Ga*," said Mercury's personal assistant Peter Freestone, "and saw thousands of hands start going. He was dazzled by that, having never seen anything quite like it before. They had only ever performed that song in darkness."

That handclap was the brainchild of *Radio Ga Ga* video director David Mallet. "I think it became the first great proof of the power of television," May said. "The first time we played this to a non-Queen audience at Live Aid, everybody knew what to do at that point. Astonishing, really. It just had to be the power of the video; there was no other way they would have known to put their hands in the air and do this double handclap thing."

What works best in the video is the use of footage from Fritz Lang's *Metropolis*. The robotic feel of the synth beats dovetails in nicely with the footage of the working class going through the drudgery of their lives. The worst part would have to be that damned flying car. The puffy-haired Deacon and May in the back seat look decidedly awkward as they look around and pretend to see the buildings nearby. Taylor is in the driver's seat yet, for some inexplicable reason, the joystick that steers the car is in the middle. "Really one of our best videos," Taylor said, "although I must admit that I find the polystyrene car a little comical."

That song was written by Roger Taylor, after being inspired by his son Felix – whose mother is French – saying "Radio Kaka". May changed it from the French word for poo, to Gaga. The song was in the same vein as The Buggles' *Video Killed the Radio Star*, albeit with a bit more hope.

Taylor's lyrics saw radio in the doldrums and was offering encouragement, saying it had yet to realise how great it could be. Still the band's new label, Capitol, was not exactly pleased their first single was seemingly about the demise of radio. "Please understand," Capitol president Jim Mazza wrote to manager Jim Beach, "that the American radio community is extremely concerned over the impact video music is having on their listenership." In the same letter, Mazza also offered some changes to the lyrics to make the song more palatable to radio. It is unclear whether Taylor took any of those suggestions on board.

Maybe the label president's ideas were a bit kaka.

6.47pm
Hammer to Fall

Ever since the Band Aid single, Geldof and Ure would joke that they were responsible for two of the worst songs ever. One of them was *Do They Know It's Christmas* and the other is the US effort it inspired, *We Are The World*.

The self-flagellation over *Do They Know It's Christmas* is unwarranted. The song still gets a run each Christmas more than 30 years later. A good chunk of those people weren't even born when the single was released. They're responding to the song, not any associated feelings of goodwill engendered by Band Aid or Live Aid.

However, when it comes to the USA for Africa effort, that criticism is justified. For *We Are the World* is truly a bad song. It had noble intentions, yes, and, it did reportedly raise more money than the UK effort, but it's still a pretty ordinary song. Critic Greil Marcus got it right when he said it sounded like a Pepsi commercial.

Lyrically, it's a very inward-looking song. In the insular way of many Americans, it's all about them. In a song inspired by people starving in another country, the most common pronoun in a song shouldn't be "we". Variations of that word appear no fewer than 10 times, compared to the just three variations of "them". It's a bad look to make yourself the focus of a charity single – it really misses the whole idea of what charity is.

Geldof was there for the recording of the US single and was not impressed with the over-the-top "showbiz" set-up. In another example of bad taste, there was a "huge feast" set up for the artists and their hangers-on. "The room was full of Hollywood fat cats and their wives eating and drinking effortlessly and talking smoothly about how wonderful it all was, this contribution to famine relief," Geldof would remember in his autobiography. "It was too much. The extremes between this room and what was happening in the studio across the hall were too great. In London, there had been the offerings of a local take-away. I left in disgust and went off into the studio."

At Wembley two songs into Queen's set, there were no signs of disgust. The crowd was well and truly into it. And Mercury was just about to prove it, doing what is now thought of as the 'Ay-Oh' bit. For roughly 40 seconds between *Radio Ga Ga* and *Hammer to Fall* he took part in a faux operatic call-and-response session with the audience.

It was nothing new for Queen fans, who had seen him do that in concerts before. Most of what Queen brought onstage was what they'd been doing in arena shows for years. The reason it was so successful and blew so many people away was that this was the first time many had been exposed to it. Most of the crowd at Wembley and watching at home were not Queen fans, they'd never shelled out the bucks for a concert ticket to one of the band's shows before. Queen may have honed their arena performance theatrics over years of playing in front of huge crowds (though official DVDs of performances in 1974 and 1975 show they hadn't gotten to that level of stagecraft at the time) but, for many, it was on display here for the first time. So it's understandable why the crowd would be so into it and why this particular show would resonate for so many years afterwards.

After *Radio Ga Ga* finishes, the crowd roars its approval. That noise, combined with the sight of the crowd seems to catch May by surprise; a smile creeps onto his face as he's seen bowing to the audience after just two songs.

Then Mercury takes over. He strolls to the front of the stage, takes a wide stance, then bursts out with an "ayyyy-Oh", swinging his right arm forward to encourage the crowd to join in. And they do. And they sound good too. Call it the harmony of the crowds; one person on their own would sound horrible but as one, the thousands of voices find the

33

right tune, pitch and timing. They all start and finish at the same time. Mercury doesn't seem to be going through the motions here either; he's really enjoying it. His call of "Alright!" at the end feels like genuine appreciation for the crowd's efforts.

Then he announces the next song – *Hammer to Fall*. It's the only time in their six-song set Mercury feels the need to do that. Maybe it's because, of the Live Aid setlist, it's the only song not to reach the top 10 (its high point on the UK charts was No13) and there's a feeling it might not be as immediately recognisable as the other tunes. It certainly had been overshadowed by The Works' earlier singles, *Radio Ga Ga* and *I Want to Break Free*.

But it was the sort of song Queen's setlist needed, tapping into the hard rock strand of their DNA, that had given birth to songs like *Stone Cold Crazy*, *Now I'm Here* and *Sheer Heart Attack* among others. It's a side of the band that had taken a back seat in the 1980s as they polished their sound to a poppy sheen.

If live performances of these songs are any indication, the band themselves got off on playing them. In video footage of these songs being played live, they are almost always faster than the version that appeared on record. That's definitely the case with *Hammer to Fall*. On the album it sounds a bit pedestrian, with a drumbeat from Taylor that seems plodding and uninterested.

But the Live Aid version, man, that rocks. Taylor's drumming is right in the pocket, May's guitar is rough with jagged edges and the harmony vocals feel vibrant and alive compared to the overproduced feel on the album.

It's not surprising this song gets the biggest crowd reaction of the set so far. If there was anyone out there resisting being swept up in the euphoria and drama of Queen's Live Aid show, this is the one that converted them. From here on the crowd just gets louder and louder as though *Hammer to Fall* flicked a switch to take the performance to the next level.

The moment from the song many remember is Mercury's dance with the cameraman. In a moment he's effectively performing for one, the cameraman who is his unwitting partner. The next he's walking off and turning to the audience with a smile on his face and a thumb pointing back over his shoulder, as if to say "how about that guy?". It's also one of the few times Deacon appears in the concert footage, when he walks towards the front of the stage, stands between Mercury and May and dances with an alarming lack of rhythm for a bass player.

Towards the end, Mercury goes into phallic mode, taking seemingly every opportunity to make out that his sawn-off microphone stand is actually a penis. Including one particular overt instance when the song reaches its … ahem … climax.

With Band Aid, Geldof's plan had been to record the single, make some money to help those starving people and get out. But the way sales of the seven-inch and 12-inch took off and surpassed his wildest expectations made him think something bigger was happening. That perhaps the feeling that BBC news story sparked in him was being felt by a lot of other people as well.

More than 3 million people in Britain alone didn't buy *Do They Know It's Christmas* just because they thought it was a good song.

"People must have tapped into this thing," he said. "What they'd seen on TV had appalled them, and they'd found no instrument to articulate that sentiment, and suddenly this silly piece of plastic came along, a fairly duff song, and that was it."

The idea to do something more, something bigger, had been percolating in Geldof's head almost immediately after the Band Aid sessions. In January he bumped into Nik Kershaw at Heathrow and mentioned the Live Aid idea; the then hit pop star signed up for it right there.

Geldof still had a Rats' album to plug so he was on the road with the band in the early part of 1985. All the while he was taking notes about how he would pull off what would become known as Live Aid. And Geldof was prepared to think big.

Organising Band Aid would seem easy compared to the huge logistical feat of setting up Live Aid. To give an example of the gargantuan task before Geldof, his promoter Harvey Goldsmith and his team, they had to convince not one, but two TV networks on two different continents to give over 17 hours of their schedule to broadcast the concert.

A couple of hours, yes, that would have seemed reasonable. But almost a whole day? No wonder Goldsmith told Geldof he was "fucking mad". At his end, Geldof thought they were making a big deal about nothing. "I never assumed that asking the BBC to clear 17 hours of TV programs would create a problem," he wrote in his autobiography.

But it was. The broadcaster initially baulked at the cost of the cancellation fees to axe shows for the day, and then the extra cost to reschedule them. Geldof hadn't seen that coming; he saw himself as giving them a day's free programming. In the US it was a bit easier; MTV came onboard. All they had to was move a day's worth of music videos for a day's worth of music. It was a no-brainer.

Geldof needed it to be on TV because he didn't envisage just raising money via ticket sales and the cash that went over the merch stalls. He wanted this to be a global telethon, where people around the world could call or mail in donations. Which made for even more work; it meant he had to make the telephone and postal arrangements for every country that would take the Live Aid broadcast – there was just no way someone from Australia could be expected to ring a UK number to pledge some money.

Then he needed to find a venue in the UK and in the US. Wembley was the obvious choice, even if they had to pay to hire it (which they did). In the US it ended up being in Philadelphia because only an east coast venue would work with the time differences.

It would be the bands who would be the easiest to deal with. Many of them would eagerly sign up to play at Wembley or John F Kennedy Stadium in Philadelphia. The UK show was so popular the only way some acts, like Duran Duran the Thompson Twins and Simple Minds, could play at Live Aid was if they flew to the US to perform. And so they did.

The perception is that it's easy for bands who appear at charity gigs; they just turn up and play. But the reality is, it costs them money. The UK bands who flew to the US paid their own way. Other acts like Paul Young and Spandau Ballet flew in from international tours. "Bands paid for rehearsals and trucking," Geldof said, "moving their stuff from coast to coast, cancelling lucrative concerts, because this was where they wanted to be."

But not everyone wanted to be there. The Rolling Stones didn't appear because, as bass player Bill Wyman told Geldof "Keith doesn't give a fuck" (though he would end up onstage in Philly with Bob Dylan). Tears for Fears were subject to a Geldof mind game where he'd announce a band was playing before they'd said okay. "Geldof thought he was so powerful that if he announced it, we'd have to say yes, or we'd look like bad people," said Curt Smith, who had planned a holiday that week after a solid year of touring.

"I was pissed off. Whether we played or not wasn't going to make a difference to the amount of money raised. So we went on holiday, because that was the only break we had."

As for Queen, it looked like they'd be another one of the bands who would choose not to appear.

6.52pm
Crazy Little Thing Called Love

Geldof would have to work to get Queen across the line. At first, he enlisted the services of Boomtown Rats keyboard player Spike Edney, who was touring with Queen, to sound them out. He asked, but the band seemed miffed Geldof hadn't approached them directly. So the Live Aid organiser tracked down manager Jim Beach, who said Mercury was fretting about his solo album at the moment. "Tell the old faggot it's going to be the biggest thing ever," Geldof retorted.

Soon after, he buttonholed May and Taylor at an awards ceremony. "I thought it would be almost impossible for him to put together," May said of Live Aid. "But I said that we were interested." Though they'd still have to work on a reluctant Mercury.

"Roger Taylor was saying he'd do it, but he didn't think Freddie would," Geldof remembered. "The band were exhausted and they were really questioning their future as well."

He finally got to put his case to Mercury, noting it was a huge event, in front of a big crowd – both at Wembley and watching at home on television. It was something virtually tailormade for someone like Mercury.

"Oh, you do have a point, Mr Geldof," Mercury said. Queen were on board.

Once they signed up, the band was honest enough to admit their decision had been driven, at least in part, by self-interest.

"Of course it is a wonderful cause and will make a pot of money for that wonderful cause," said Taylor.

"But make no mistake – we're doing this for our own glory as well.

"Let's not lie, don't tell me there was one act there that wasn't aware that there would be more than a billion people watching."

Mercury, the one who had dragged the chain on the Live Aid decision, had similar feelings. He wasn't taking to the stage at Wembley out of guilt over the situation in Ethiopia. His motivation was much more personal.

"I'm doing it out of pride," he said. "Pride that I've been asked as well as that I actually can do something like that.

"So basically I'm doing it out of a feeling that one way all the hard work that I've actually done over the years has paid off, because they're actually asking me to do something to be proud of."

Much has been made of the fact that Queen chose to make the Live Aid performance a greatest hits package. "Geldof called Live Aid a jukebox," May said, "so it seemed obvious to simply play the hits and get off."

Mercury agreed with that assessment, noting it wasn't a "promotional thing"; "you're not trying to put across your new material or anything like that, you're playing songs that people identify with."

But a quick look at the setlists for that July day in Wembley would put paid to the notion that Queen were the only ones who had that idea. Ultravox's four-song set was nothing but hits – three of them had been top 10 singles. The Who and Elton John went into their back catalogue to bring out their hits as well. Sting, Dire Straits and top of the poppers Nik Kershaw and Spandau Ballet did the same thing.

What made Queen's six-song set different was that they turned it into a medley of sorts. They cut out all the gap between the songs; the short chat with the audience before *Crazy Little Thing Called Love* is the only time in the set that happens (the "Ah-Oh!" call-and-response isn't a chat with the crowd, more a part of the performance). And they shortened some of the songs as well. That's why they could fit six songs into their 20 minutes on stage.

Taking that approach would mean Queen couldn't just turn up on the day and reel off the songs one after the other. If they were going to play a sort-of medley, they'd have to rehearse.

So they booked three days in London's Shaw

Theatre to work out which songs to include and then structure the medley so they had it down pat. They even took measures to ensure they didn't run over time. "I went out and bought some electric clocks," said roadie Peter Hince. "We had them wired up and in front of the stage, so we could check to see when our time was up."

Harvey Goldsmith had the same idea for the Live Aid show. The day before, he went out and bought around 30 clocks and mounted them everywhere backstage; at times in the concert footage, you can see them mounted on the wall in the wings of the Wembley stage. Given the times of the Wembley performance had to mesh in with what was happening in Philadelphia, it was crucial bands didn't run over their allotted time. "I sent notes round to every single act," Goldsmith said, "saying 'I don't care what time you go on, I only care what time you go off'." To help them out, there was a traffic light system that, glowed amber when they had to get off and, they wouldn't see the red light because the power would be cut.

Something else would be cut during the Queen set – the telecast. American viewers watching Live Aid on MTV watched an ad break at this point. While the band played *Crazy Little Thing Called Love*, America saw seven ads, including ones for Chevrolet, Pepsi, Foot Locker and English Leather.

The ad break is so long that by the time MTV returns to the coverage the four-minute slot of *Crazy Little Thing Called Love* has come and gone, and Queen has moved onto *We Will Rock You*.

American viewers only got to hear that song in the background as MTV VJ Nina Blackwood introduces a pre-recorded interview with Marilyn McCoo (a singer known in America and almost nowhere else). To cut this song from the US coverage was odd; *Crazy Little Thing Called Love* was a hit in America and the only US No1 in the band's Live Aid setlist.

The song's exclusion from the US telecast is likely the reason behind why the drive to class Queen as the best band at Live Aid comes from the UK and not the US. It also explains the very belated rush of American music publications to validate the band's performance when the *Bohemian Rhapsody* film was released. In 1985, American audiences did not get the uninterrupted Queen performance. Instead, at the time and for years afterwards, America would have a different opinion as to who was the best on the day.

Anyone who got the BBC feed of the show got to see Queen perform was really was the outlier of the set. The other tunes were operatic, dramatic or bombastic; but *Crazy Little Thing Called Love* is a relatively lightweight pop song by comparison. What it does in the Live Aid set is provide a bit of light relief, some fun rockabilly.

At 2.42 minutes it's a short song for a band known to routinely push past the four-minute mark. It also had a remarkably short timespan between idea and recording – four hours. In 1979, Mercury had just arrived in Munich with roadie Hince, where the band had some loose plans to record their next album. The pair checked into the Hilton and Mercury went to take a bath.

Minutes later, he yelled for Hince to bring him a guitar. In the hotel room, dripping wet and wrapped in towels, the frontman would pick out the rhythm he had in his head. "*Crazy Little Thing Called Love* took me five, 10 minutes to write," Mercury said. "I was restricted by only knowing a few chords. It's a good discipline as I simply had to write in a small framework."

He took it to the studio and ran through the song with Taylor and Deacon, taking advantage of May's absence because he figured the guitarist would hate the song. They laid down a backing track which would remain on the finished song.

Mercury was right about May; he was no fan of the tune. But the song was done and dusted by that stage and May realised he had to get some guitar on it quick smart. That caused some more friction, as producer Mack told May to use a Telecaster instead of his much-loved Red Special. "I wasn't happy," May remembered. "I kicked against it, but I saw that it was the right way to go."

In just a few hours, the band had written and recorded what would be a No1 hit in four countries – and their first in the United States.

At the end of *Hammer to Fall*, Mercury walked to the side of the stage, giving a hug to the camera crew he'd danced with a minute or so earlier. Then he reached out to a roadie and took possession of a milky-coffee coloured Telecaster.

Walking back to the microphone he tinkers and

tunes the guitar strumming it with sharp muted strokes. Mercury gets to centre stage and directly addresses the crowd for the first and only time in Queen's set. "This next song is only dedicated to beautiful people here tonight. That means all of you. Thank you for coming along … and making this a great occasion."

He strums the first chords of *Crazy Little Thing Called Love*. It takes the crowd a few seconds to recognise the tune, and they give it the most muted response of any song in the set. Who knows, maybe they're still catching their breath from the arena rock of *Hammer to Fall*.

The crowd catch their breath soon enough, raising their hands in the air to clap along with Taylor's snare drum. By the time May's guitar solo is finished, they're eager to accept Mercury's invitation to sing a few lines on their own. And when the band ends the tune on a rising crescendo, the crowd cheers the whole way.

It wasn't a Queen audience when they started but by this time there are surely more than a few converts in the crowd. And watching at home.

6.55pm
We Will Rock You

If you've got a stadium full of rock stars, it's not surprising that a few helicopters were involved. While some bands, including Queen, chose to be driven to Wembley, others took advantage of a helicopter ride. UK TV presenter Noel Edmonds had a copter company at the time and ended up flying some of the

Live Aid talent to a cricket oval a few hundred yards from Wembley.

A cricket oval that was hosting the final that day. Umpires would cast their eyes skyward every now and then; if they saw a helicopter drawing near, they'd blow a whistle and the players would leave the field so it could land. That night the venue would host a wedding reception and the father of the bride would get angry at the constant helicopter intrusion. So David Bowie was sent over to patch things up.

The Thin White Duke was one of those performers who took a helicopter ride to Wembley that day. His management told Edmonds Bowie only travelled in helicopters that were blue on the inside. After some effort, a helicopter fitting those specifications was found.

"I was killing time with him at Battersea [where Edmonds' helicopter company was located] before he flew in and I said 'look at the inside of this helicopter!', Edmonds said.

"He looked at me as if I were mad. He didn't give a shit what colour the helicopter was."

Bowie was partly responsible for one of the show-stopping moments at Live Aid. After playing a four-song set where it seemed like he and his band were having one big party onstage, Bowie introduced a harrowing short film that showed the poor and starving in Ethiopia. He was meant to play a fifth song at Live Aid but had decided to give that up so the film could be screened at Wembley.

Set to the sound of The Cars' *Drive*, it turned the Wembley crowd dead silent as they watched small starving children crying out in desperate hunger, or putting their head in their hands in a gesture of futility they should have been too young to know about.

The short video had been filmed by the Canadian Broadcasting Corporation, who managed to get Geldof to sit still for a minute and watch it. "It was a short sequence of a child, weakened by hunger, trying and trying again to stand up on his little matchstick legs," Geldof said.

"They had edited it over The Cars' *Drive*. The juxtaposition was bizarre. The child's pitiful courage turned the poignancy of the song into a profound sadness. Who's gonna pick you up when you fall?

"My eyes filled with tears and my voice caught in my throat. 'We've got to have this, lads, for the day'."

It was just one example of some of the other things

going on, aside from Queen that day. Because, in the wake of the *Bohemian Rhapsody* movie, there is this focus on Queen's set to the detriment of everything else that happened onstage that day.

There were 20 other performances that day; some of them were great, some not so good and at least one unfairly maligned. That last one was Adam Ant's one-song set. He was only there because he shared the same manager as Sting – Miles Copeland. Geldof called Copeland, hoping to get Sting to commit to bring The Police to Live Aid.

Copeland said "hey, what about Adam Ant?" and Geldof said yes, hoping it would curry favour with Sting for that Police reunion. That reunion never happened, but Geldof still had to find a spot for Adam Ant. The smart move would have been for him to use his one-song slot to perform *Ant Music* or some other hit from his back catalogue. Instead, he opted for his latest single *Vive Le Rock*. Few in the crowd had heard it, and it showed.

Promoter Goldsmith said Ant's performance "didn't work at all". "He looked out of sorts with the time, and didn't fit in." Watching Ant's performance, he certainly gives it a red-hot go; with the running around onstage and the high kicks, he's easily the most animated performer of the day. So much so that he ends up short of breath for the final verse.

The song itself is alright – the live version is far better than what he would release as a single. But the charts would show his best days were behind him and he was the sole instance of Geldof going against his plan to only book artists who would pull a crowd.

Speaking of Geldof, of course his band got a spot on the stage. Seriously, would anyone expect the guy to go to all the trouble of organising this colossal event and then not book his own band? The Rats played three songs – though the only one most of the audience would recognise was *I Don't Like Mondays*. It was band's biggest hit so Geldof knew they had to play it, despite how he felt about it. "There had been a time when I grew to despise the song because we had to sing it so often that it began to feel cheapened by the repetition," he said.

Right after the line "the lesson today is how to die", Geldof had arranged for the band to stop and he raised his clenched fist into the air. It was meant as a big dramatic statement, and the crowd responded that way, but looking back at it now it does seem a bit naff.

Midge Ure, the other songwriter behind *Do They Know it's Christmas*, also made the stage at Wembley. In his case it wasn't due to favouritism; his band was riding high on a series of UK hits at the time. Aside from *Vienna*, none of the others would have travelled well outside England though.

Sting had resisted Geldof's entreaties to call Andy and Stewart and get The Police back together. Also, despite having released his debut solo album *Dream of the Blue Turtles*, he would play no songs from that release. Instead, he would play four Police songs in a seven-song set, joined at one point by Phil Collins.

Midge Ure suggested Sting was planning to play with his new band, but they asked to be paid just before they were to walk onstage. "Sting told them to fuck off and walked on with just an acoustic guitar," Ure wrote in his autobiography. It's an interesting story, implying that Sting changed his set for the biggest show in his career as he walked to the microphone. But there seems to be a few holes in it.

For one, Sting's guitar is electric and not acoustic. Also, if he ditched his band at the last minute, why is all their equipment not set up onstage? The only instrument behind Sting is the piano Collins will play for a few tunes. Sting might have ditched his band for Live Aid but, if he did it was early enough that the roadies could take all the gear off stage.

Sade was the real surprise packet from Wembley. Their cool jazz stylings were right at home in tiny smoky nightclub where 20-somethings convince themselves they're sophisticated. That sound should have failed dismally on the huge Wembley stage at three o'clock in the afternoon, but dammit, if they didn't make it work. Instead of being overwhelmed by the large stage and the huge crowd before them, the band managed to shrink it down to an intimate venue.

Elvis Costello was one of the performers who had to keep making way for others. He was originally slated to play three songs, but that number kept getting cut. When his manager told him he was now down to one song, Costello reportedly said if they were going to cut any more songs he wouldn't play at all.

If his three songs had been left alone and he'd been able to patch things up with the just-broken-up Attractions, Costello could have had a barnstorming set. Imagine the likes of *Pump It Up* and *Oliver's Army* on the Live Aid stage.

As it was Costello went to the microphone for one song, and it wasn't even his. In the video footage of his performance, you can see what appears to be the song lyrics written on the back on his hand. That suggests his decision to perform this particular song was a last-minute one, rather than something he'd rehearsed ahead of schedule.

He introduces it as "an old northern English folk song", before offering some jangly, yet slightly familiar chords on his electric guitar. It's not until Costello gets to the end of the first line that the audience erupts in recognition – it's *The Beatles' All You Need Is Love*.

It's a winner with the crowd, which immediately starts clapping along and even doing the "do-do-do-dedo" harmonies in the chorus. Costello had picked the right song, and coupled it with a simple, understated performance that was a refreshing from the superficial hipster fashion show that was Spandau Ballet who had just left the stage.

Spandau Ballet, like Nik Kershaw and Paul Young, were on the bill because they were moving plenty of units at the time. That's why the actual list of artists who played Live Aid hasn't stood the test of time; Geldof wasn't looking for the most significant, artistically worthy acts to play at Live Aid, he wanted the bands who would draw punters in by the truckload. Live Aid was about raking in as much money for charity as possible, not trying to show how cool his musical tastes were. That said, there were some icons at Live Aid; David Bowie, The Who, Elton John. And of course Queen, who are just about to play a song explicitly written with an audience in mind.

Unless you're a hardcore fan of a band, no-one ever remembers the B-side of a single. These days, there are surely people who don't remember singles at all. Back in the days before online streaming made them largely pointless, bands would release what they figured would be their next hit on a single.

Because a single had two sides, it meant the band had to put something on the other side. Sometimes, that was a deep cut from the same album. Other times it would be a song that was recorded during the album session and didn't make the cut but, to mollify the songwriter, it was given a brief life as a B-side.

But no-one really paid them much attention; they were largely there to fill up space. Which makes *We Will Rock You* an oddity; it was a B-side (though, not in the US, where they put out as a double A-side. America may not have understood Queen, but they got this right). Taylor said the plan was always to release them together, but *We Will Rock You* wouldn't be able to carry the A-side expectations.

"Always wanted them to be together, they just seem to work together," Taylor told Billboard. "*We Will Rock You*, we didn't think was a single. We almost saw it like an introduction to *We Are The Champions*, which is a more classic, very grand song.

"We were very aware that we didn't want to be labelled as a glam rock/prog rock dinosaur, so we wanted to absolutely consciously change and we tried to keep changing."

Though judging by the video for *Rock*, the band may not have expected the song to be the monster it turned out to be. The band look thoroughly miserable and cold on a makeshift stage in the snow of Taylor's backyard. Even Mercury looks like he can't be bothered putting in any effort.

May, who wrote the song with Mercury, said the video was dashed off after filming one for *Spread Your Wings* (which has the same snowy set-up but the band look far more into it – as does the cameraman). And he wasn't happy about it; he felt the band was underestimating his song.

"In the little bit of time we had left – an hour – we shot it and our noses were all red because it was freezing cold," May said. "There weren't more than a couple takes and nothing to really go with. I took the video to the studio and edited the fuck out of it and made a cut on every beat and used all the close-ups I could to make it spring to life. It was a makeshift video that says nothing about the song."

The pairing of the songs was reflected on the *News of the World* album; *Rock* led that off, followed by *Champions*. And there was a minimal gap between the two tunes, very much hinting the band saw them as two parts of a single song.

For a short period of time, the band would revert to the "fast" version of *We Will Rock You*; an odd decision for a song that, in its original form, was designed for audience interaction. "Freddie and I thought it would be an interesting experiment to write songs with audience participation specifically in mind," May said of the original version of the song.

It was crowds in two different venues that inspired May. The first was a gig at Bingley Hall near Birmingham during the band's 1977 tour. "They would sing all the songs," May said. "In a place like Birmingham, they'd be so vociferous that we'd have to stop the show and let them sing to us." The second gig was at the old Boston Garden and its wooden beams and floor. "When the crowd made noise during the encore it was like thunder," May remembered. "That sound I heard was in my head and the only question was how to make it in the studio."

Well, for a start, you don't use instruments. It's just voice and guitar on the album version. The band stamped on wooden boards in the old church where they were recording; stamping twice and clapping once. May recorded that over and over to build up the sound to make it sound like a choir of stomping, adding a slight delay to some of the recording so it sounds like a huge crowd.

As for the words, aside from the one-line chorus,

they're actually not about a band pledging to rock anyone. They're about the three stages of life; the subject starts out with as a child with mud on his face, grows to a man full of aggression, and then ends up an old man full of regret who now just wants a simple life.

The audience interaction element would have a surprise spin-off that fuelled the song's longevity. Sporting teams – particularly those in the US where all the major sports have lots of gaps where no sport is being played – worked out the song was a winner when blasted from the big PA in their home arena. Music provided a great way to keep the atmosphere upbeat when nothing was happening on-court, and a song like *We Will Rock You* encouraged fans in the bleachers to become participants rather than observers.

That's just what the audience becomes at Live Aid. Mercury slung his guitar over his shoulder, walked to the side of the stage and handed it over to a roadie. Unlike the other songs in the Live Aid set, the audience don't need to hear a bit before they work out what's coming. It takes just a few beats of Taylor drums for them to recognise what's coming and the loud cheers that greeted the end of *Crazy Little Thing Called Love* get louder still.

May kicks in with a clean, loud guitar riff as the crowd raises their hands and claps in time to the beat – even though they clap on the "stomping" beats as well. Mercury sings the first verse and then sits back and lets the crowd choir take centre stage for the chorus – and they're *loud*.

One verse and one chorus are all they get. *We Will Rock You* is one of the songs to get edited down in the pursuit of a jukebox medley. All-up it runs for one minute and 15 seconds – around half the time of the album version.

Not that the audience feels in any way short-changed. By this point, they're totally enjoying this ride.

6.56pm
We Are the Champions

Today, the accepted wisdom is that Queen owned the Live Aid stage, that no-one else came close. But as someone who was around to see Live Aid (albeit on TV), my recollection is somewhat different. Straight after Live Aid, the band everyone seemed to be talking about wasn't Queen but four guys from Ireland – U2. Granted part of that may have been because "everyone" was largely the US media, where the Queen set was sliced in the middle by the broadcaster's need to show a stack of ads, but still, the belief that Queen ruled the roost is one that has been formed in hindsight.

That the U2 performance was such a success came as a surprise to the band members themselves. They'd thought they had screwed up on a worldwide stage – and not because of Bono's immense mullet.

They went on two slots before Queen – the two big acts sandwiched the ever-dull Dire Straits. U2 had released *The Unforgettable Fire* and was making real headway into the US market and there was the thought the Live Aid show would push them to the next level (though confusion exists about whether or not they threatened not to show. Geldof said he got a call from someone with the band saying they wouldn't play if they couldn't have a soundcheck. Geldof said "fine, don't come". U2's manager Paul McGuinness says that claim is "bollocks").

So it was a real disappointment for the band that they messed up their performance so badly they only played two of the planned three songs. The song they didn't play? Just their big hit at the time *Pride (In The Name of Love)*.

They started out so well, launching their set with *Sunday Bloody Sunday* – one of their biggest hits to date. People like to say someone in Queen's camp tinkered with the limiters on the desk so their sound was louder and better than everyone else's, but U2's sound is pretty good on *Sunday, Bloody Sunday*.

Then Bono introduces the second song, *Bad* – an apt choice given how the band will later judge their performance. It's a song that goes for more than 11 minutes – a decent segment of that featuring no vocals.

The song – about the scourge of heroin – isn't a barnstormer. Instead, it's a slow burner and you can see the audience gradually getting into it (and perhaps, having been on their feet for hours at a rock festival, they welcome the occasional slow song). About six minutes in – though the song is working so well it doesn't feel like six minutes have passed – Bono decides to go for a wander. Which is where all the trouble begins. In what comes across as a real prima donna move, he drops the microphone to the stage and walks off to the right.

There he leaps down into the photo pit at the front of the stage and begins making beckoning gestures to the crowd, as if he wants them all to push forward. He starts pointing to each person that security is dragging over the crash barrier below him, gesturing he wants them brought to him. But of course security have bigger things to deal with that some rock star, so they ignore him.

Bono continues to point and beckon to the crowd before suddenly deciding to leap out of the photo pit and down to the crowd. He gestures to security to bring the next person they drag over the barrier to him, seemingly overlooking the fact loads of people are now being jammed in because Bono first called them forward and is now standing a foot or two away.

That next person over is a woman (no surprise there, all the people getting dragged over at this point in U2's set are women). She's 15-year-old Kal Khalique, who was there with her sister to see Wham!. Bono gives her a big hug and then starts dancing with her to the music the rest of his band is playing (keep in mind they're all up on the stage and can't see what's going on).

Bono would later suggest he was concerned about people being crushed, but he had a track record of pulling people out of the crowd to create a "moment". And that's what he did here; he tried so hard to get security to bring him a woman and once they did, he danced with her for few seconds before walking away. Though not before all the cameras caught it.

He climbs back up to the photo pit and, lo and behold, there are sisters Melanie and Elaine Hill, the two women who had been lifted over the barrier but not brought to him.

They both get a hug and kiss before being taken back down to the crowd. Then Bono calls for the mic and starts singing for the first time in almost two minutes, much to the relief of the band. Drummer Larry Mullen Jr had spent the Bono-less time wondering how long they could keep playing what was a very simple musical part. "It was kind of excruciating," he said. "We didn't know whether we should stop, we didn't know where he was, we didn't know if he'd fallen."

Guitarist The Edge was similarly confused as to what was happening below their eyeline. "He was gone for so long I started to think maybe he had decided to end the set early and was on his way to the dressing room," he said. "I was totally thrown, and I'm looking at Adam and Larry to see if they know what's going on and they're looking back at me with complete panic across their faces.

"I'm just glad the cameras didn't show the rest of the band during the whole drama, because we must have looked like the Three Stooges up there."

Missing the chance to play *Pride*, and being left out onstage like a trio of stooges, the band lit into Bono backstage. "We didn't do the hit because I'd gone AWOL to try and find a television moment and forgotten about the song," Bono said. "The band were very, very upset – they nearly fired me." Mullen felt the band had blown "an opportunity to be great".

They went home to lick their wounds and Bono fell into a bit of a funk about letting the band down. A few days after the performance they started hearing that, far from being a mess, the U2 set was being spoken of as one of the standouts of the day.

"It really took us by surprise when people started talking about U2 as one of the noteworthy performances of the day," Edge said. "I thought they were joking. I really thought we were crap." Manager McGuinness said it was one of the biggest things to happen to the band – all four of their albums went back into the UK charts the week after Live Aid and that image of Bono dancing with Khalique boosted their profile worldwide.

The other notable performers on the bill that day were heading into their last song – the companion piece to *We Will Rock You*. Mercury returned the piano where he started the set around 15 minutes earlier, and plays the first notes of *We Are The Champions*. A few lines later, his voice soars as the rest of the band join in, as though he doesn't need a microphone at all to reach the crowd. It might go against the accepted wisdom of hitting them with a rocker as your closing tune, but the anthemic *We Are the Champions* is a perfect choice. But that was something Queen had well and truly worked out by this point; the song had been the regular closer in their sets for around five years by this time.

The pronoun at the start of the song title doesn't denote the four people onstage, but reaches out to envelop all the people in the crowd – who have their arms up and swaying in slow harmony – and all the people at home. It strikes the perfect note of inclusiveness at a concert where the world has come together to help out some of its people.

It's a feeling that pours cold water on the claims that the song is arrogant and self-absorbed. From its earliest days the song was meant as a way of joining the band and the audience as one. "I was thinking about football when I wrote it", Mercury would explain. "I wanted a participation song, something the fans could latch onto."

In that way it is the partner of *We Will Rock You*; both tunes are written to include a part for the audience.

As May, Deacon and Taylor drive the end of the song to a high point, Mercury blows the crowd a kiss and waves. He lets the band go on for a while longer before raising his arm in the air and swinging it down to signal the end of the set. The crowd roars its thanks and approval; it's the loudest the place has been that day.

The four members walk to the front of the stage, as though this is their show, and bow. Mercury says

"So long, Wembley! We love you!" and they walk from the stage, leaving the likes of David Bowie, The Who and Elton John to wonder, 'How the hell are we supposed to follow *that*?"

9.47pm
Is This the World We Created?

Let us pause and spare a thought for the quiet one – John Deacon. Always the least interested in the spotlight, at Live Aid he passed on the chance to be introduced to Prince Charles and Lady Diana, instead sending his roadie in his place. "I thought I'd make a fool of myself [if I went]," Deacon explained.

In the Queen set that day, the played seven songs (if you count this duo by May and Mercury). Three were Mercury's, two came from May's pen and one was written by Taylor. Deacon? Well, he missed out – not one of the Queen tunes were penned by him.

It's not as though he didn't have many tunes in his quiver – *You're My Best Friend*, *Another One Bites the Dust*, (credited as the band's best-selling single worldwide), *I Want to Break Free* and co-writes like *Under Pressure*. But, being the quiet one, he went with the flow – but it's not hard to imagine the crowd totally losing it if they had heard 30-odd seconds of *Another One Bites the Dust* and its iconic bassline.

The first half of the 1980s hadn't been ideal for Queen. A huge act in the 1970s, the new decade found them struggling at times. Things started well, with the 1980 release of *The Game*, which spawned two US No1 singles in *Crazy Little Thing Called Love* and *Another One Bites the Dust*.

At the end of 1980, they released their soundtrack to the movie *Flash Gordon*. At the time it was a bit of a misstep. The movie itself bombed, unable to decide if it was supposed to be serious or campy. The poor reception rubbed off on Queen, whose soundtrack album was less successful on the charts than *The Game*. The latter album went to No1 in both the UK and US, while the *Flash Gordon* soundtrack could do no better than 10th in its home market and 23 in the US.

Recent history has been kinder to the movie; its obvious campiness has seen it develop a cult fanbase. As for the soundtrack, while many fans seem to downgrade it, Queen pulled together a pretty good album – the addition of dialogue from the movie adds a storyline and sense of drama to it.

But, as far as Queen releases go, the weirdest was yet to come. If fans were cool on the *Flash Gordon* soundtrack, then they were positively icy upon the release of 1982's *Hot Space*. It took Mercury and Deacon's interest in funk and the club sounds so far as to make it unrecognisable as a Queen album. Instead it felt like a Mercury solo album. The passage of time hasn't been kind to *Hot Space*; today its electronic-heavy songs sound dated and some songs, like *Staying Power,* are actually quite terrible. Even Queen seem keen to avoid it; when it comes to the band's greatest hits packages, songs from *Hot Space* are thin on the ground.

There had been friction within the band throughout the 1980s, due to the heavy touring and recording schedule. But it was the sharp left-turn of *Hot Space* that brought things to a head. Calling the album "a mistake", May said he was glad to finish touring it. "I didn't feel that this tour was making me very happy," he said. "The last night in Los Angeles, I felt quite cheered up. I was prepared to think 'well, I really don't want to do this anymore'."

He wasn't the only one; in 1983 the band took a break from touring – and from each other. Mercury, for one, was sick of the album-tour-album-tour rut the band had been in for a decade. "It's like a painter," he said. "You paint away and then you stand back and look at it in perspective. That's exactly what we needed. We just needed to be away from each other, otherwise you just keep going in that routine and you don't even know if you're going down."

So they all went off and worked on solo projects. Well, except Deacon, who probably stayed at home with his family and enjoyed waking up in his own bed on a regular basis. The most recognised solo project was Mercury's *Mr Bad Guy* album, which would take almost three years to finish and see release just months before Live Aid. By that time, the band was well and truly back together (and perhaps Mercury had been taken down a peg or two when his solo album didn't perform as well as a Queen release).

Today's narrative with Queen's Live Aid show is that they were a fading icon; they weren't having hits and no-one really cared about them anymore. It's a story that utterly ignores the success of *The Works* album. After a year apart, the band got back together to work on that album. Released in February 1984, *The Works* would reach No2 on the UK charts and spawn three top 10 singles – three of which (if you count this song) the band figured were worthy of appearing on the Live Aid setlist. They certainly weren't a band with their best moments in the rear-view mirror, as far as songwriting and chart success went.

It's true there was a possibility of breaking up,

though more out of boredom and fatigue than anything else. "I think they were at a low ebb," remembered roadie Peter Hince. "I didn't think they'd definitely break up but it was more like, 'Well, what are they going to do next?'."

Well, performing in front of millions upon millions of people and stealing the show would be one option.

This song is one that often gets forgotten when people talk about the Queen Live Aid performance. Mercury and May would return to the stage, nearly three hours after Queen's star turn. They would perform for four minutes at the pointy end of the proceedings; only Paul McCartney and an all-in rendition of *Do They Know It's Christmas* would follow them.

"It looks as if we wrote *Is This The World We Created* for this event," Mercury said in an interview during a break in rehearsals, "but we didn't. Although it seems to fit the bill."

That would be because it was written about the very same famine in Africa that inspired Live Aid. It was a last-minute addition to the album; May said they'd been axing tracks because there wasn't enough room. Then producer Mack said there was a small space left on the record, so go and write something. So May and Mercury went off into a corner with an acoustic guitar and "the whole business of Africa in our minds," after seeing a news story of the African tragedy.

At Live Aid Mercury and May would walk onstage, the singer carrying his cut-off mic stand and wearing all white, May in jeans and a collared shirt with the sleeves cut off. Curiously, they're wearing the same sneaker – was there a two for one deal at the store?

Befitting the slow, delicate nature of the song the pair perform it while sitting on stools – they'd already won the crowd over a few hours earlier, they can afford to take it easy now. Mercury mugs to the crowd for a little while before suddenly deciding to get in the right mood for the song. May is to his left and noodling on his acoustic guitar waiting for a nod from Mercury to signal he's finished with his mugging and is ready to go. Always the performer, Mercury can't stay seated for long. He rises for the first chorus and stays on his feet for the rest of the song.

As a performance it's not riveting or spellbinding like Queen's earlier set. Also, it goes against Geldof's idea that bands should treat it like a global jukebox and play the hits, the songs people recognise. Is *This The World We Created* certainly didn't fit that bill; outside of Queen fans few in the crowd would have recognised the tune.

But the crowd doesn't seem to care; just as Mercury finishes the final notes, the whistles and cheers start to erupt from Wembley.

"Thank you very much," Mercury says as he blows the crowd a kiss and he and May walk off the stage.

9.57pm
The Finale

After that duo, Paul McCartney would perform one song too – *Let It Be*. It was a coup for Geldof, who'd felt the Live Aid bill needed at least one Beatle on it. And it was a big deal to get McCartney, who had all but given up on live performances since disbanding Wings in 1980. His kids had to cajole their nervous dad into taking part.

He would start the opening piano chord in darkness, getting to the third line before the spotlight found him. Microphone issues meant that, while those watching on TV around the world could hear McCartney singing, those at Wembley were treated to an instrumental for almost two minutes.

Watching video of the performance, you can pinpoint when the problem is rectified – the crowd lets out a cheer that doesn't correspond to anything happening onstage. If McCartney was aware of the problem he may have been thinking "see, I knew I shouldn't have gotten back onstage". Or maybe not; in that video he sure seems to be enjoying himself.

A chorus made up of Geldof, Alison Moyett, Pete Townsend, David Bowie and Midge Ure would join McCartney onstage. And muff their first line – mistakenly thinking they're at the chorus and singing "Let it be" over the top of McCartney, who has just gone into a verse. When they get the words right, their performance isn't much better. If only *their* mics weren't working.

After Sir Paul, members of Queen would get to sing the song they missed out on at Christmas last year. The finale to Live Aid at Wembley was a massed chorus of *Do They Know It's Christmas*, with some members holding the lyric sheets that had been copied at the last minute because some of the artists didn't know the words.

Taylor is there, sporting sunglasses at night. Mercury appears in the crowd about halfway through next to U2's Bono, who he apparently chatted up backstage.

"I was up against a wall and he put his hand on the wall, Bono remembered, "and was talking to me like he was chatting up a chick." The U2 frontman had to be told later that Mercury was gay – somehow he didn't already know that. Mercury even leans in over Bono's shoulder to reach the mic during one of the choruses.

The curly head of May appears on camera amongst the crowd right near the end of the song. It's hardly surprising that Deacon is nowhere to be seen. If the retiring bassplayer is onstage he's right at the edges, avoiding the limelight and the cameras.

Or who knows, maybe he's not at Wembley at all. Perhaps he packed up after Queen's set and headed home.

The Live Aid concerts were estimated to have made as much as £150 million, on top of the £8 million pulled in by the single. While many would be left feeling good that they'd helped the starving, the money raised would go on to cause controversy.

Early deliveries of food sat on the docks at Ethiopia because, critics said, the Live Aid Trust didn't think about how the supplies would be transported to the hungry. So they used some of the funds to buy a fleet of trucks, which further delayed the delivery of aid.

In 1986 *Spin* magazine went to Ethiopia to see where the money went. Much of it apparently ended up in the hands of the country's dictator Mengistu, who used it to buy weapons from the Russians. His people were still hungry but now he had the best-equipped military on the continent.

That army according to Spin, was using the food to lure people into resettlement camps, which were not welcoming places. "Those who have escaped to refugee camps in Sudan," Spin reporter Robert Keating wrote, "tell horror stories of being beaten, being shot trying to escape, or of watching their families separated and brutalised."

Geldof declined repeated offers to comment on

the story before publication, but would respond a month later. His response focused on comments made by aid organisation Medecins Sans Frontieres, even though they were only one of a number of sources in the story.

"This is a politically fraught area of the Horn of Africa," Geldof's statement read, "therefore, subject to misinformational campaigns constantly perpetrated by the interested parties in Ethiopia, Tigre, and Eritrea. Most probably consciously abetted by outside agencies and now unfortunately and almost certainly innocently, MSF seems to have allowed itself to be used as pawns."

Others have criticised Live Aid and other fundraisers of their ilk for perpetuating an image of Africa as being full of starving children with flies buzzing around their faces. An apocalyptic continent of famine and misery, with the western world playing the role of the great saviour.

The criticism would not stop Geldof, who would organise new versions of *Do They Know It's Christmas* in 1989, 2004 and 2014. He would also set up the Live 8 concerts in July 2005. Rather than raising money directly, the shows were part of a campaign to get governments to increase the amount of aid they sent to Africa.

As for Queen, well Live Aid proved to be a shot of adrenaline for a band who was sick of the whole thing. "We were so jaded by that point," Taylor says of the feeling before Live Aid. "We didn't think we'd tour again for five years, if at all – we'd just had it."

By September 1985, they were back in the studio. The first release from those sessions would be *One Vision* – which would go onto become a live favourite – and a new album in *A Kind of Magic*. That long player would reach No1 on the UK album. If that wasn't enough of a sign that Queen was back, then their appearance at Wembley was. Almost exactly a year to the day they rocked that arena at Live Aid, the band returned to show that it hadn't been a fluke. The double live album from one of those shows went to No1 all over the place and sold like gangbusters. It went platinum in at least nine countries.

A pall on the band's second wind would come just three years after Live Aid, when Mercury was diagnosed with HIV. But the singer would work to keep the news of his diagnosis limited to the band, family and close friends. And he kept working, Queen would release two more albums. In November 1991, he would make a formal announcement that he had AIDS and passed away less than 24 hours later.

But Queen would live on – just a year later *Bohemian Rhapsody* got a new lease of life via the film *Wayne's World*. The long-running musical *We Will Rock You* came in 2002, while in 2004 the band went back on the road with Paul Rodgers on vocals.

In 2009, the bad would find a better fit both vocally and in attitude through *American Idol* runner-up Adam Lambert. The year 2018 would see a further boost to Queen's profile – and more recognition for their Live Aid show – with the release of the film *Bohemian Rhapsody*.

Those 17-odd minute on stage at Live Aid in 1985 had a long-running effect for decades that few could have predicted.

Bibliography

Blake, Mark, *Freddie Mercury: A Kind of Magic*, Backbeat, 2016

Blake, Mark, *Is This the Real Life*, Aurum Press, 2011

Geldof, Bob, *Is That It*, Ballentine, 1988

Hince, Peter, *Queen Unseen: My Life with the Greatest Rock Band of the 20th Century*, Music Press Books, 2016

Inglis, Ian (ed), *Performance and Popular Music: History, Place and Time*, Ashgate, 2006

Jones, Dylan, *The Eighties: One Day, One Decade*, Windmill Books, 2014

Jones, Lesley-Anne, *Bohemian Rhapsody: The Definitive Biography of Freddie Mercury*, Hodder, 2012

Maconie, Stuart, *The People's Songs: The Story of Modern Britain in 50 Songs*, Ebury Press, 2014

Popoff, Martin, *Queen Album by Album*, Voyageur Press, 2018

Purvis, Georg, *Queen: Complete Works*, Titan Publishing, 2018

Tannenbaum, Rob, and Marks, Craig, *I Want My MTV: The Uncensored Story of the Music Video Revolution*, Penguin, 2011

Ure, Midge, *If I Was: The Autobiography*, Virgin, 2004

If you liked this book why not check out my others, all which are available through my micropublishing company Last Day of School? (www.lastdayofschool.net)

The Slab
24 Stories of Beer in Australia

Beer. You know it and, chances are, you love it. But you
might not know the part beer has played in Australian history.
Right from the start beer was there. It was on board The
Endeavour when Captain Cook set sail for Australia. It was
drunk not long after the First Fleet landed in Botany Bay.
It was there when World War I soldiers got a skinful and ran
riot in the streets of Sydney. It was there during the era of six
o'clock closing where people were still drinking it long after
the little hand had passed the six. It was even there when it
really shouldn't have been - when Canberra declared itself an
alcohol-free zone.

What? You didn't know the nation's capital used to be dry?
Well, then you need this book. You'll also find out just what
the hell Voltron has to do with Victoria Bitter.

*"History as it should be written. With beer. About beer. Crisp.
Refreshing. Won't cause bloat."*
John Birmingham, author of Leviathan

James Squire: The Biography

After getting caught swiping a few chickens from a neighbour, James Squire was sentenced to seven years in Sydney Cove. You could say it was the best thing he ever did – it led to him become a brewer, policeman, property tycoon, respected citizen and a bloody rich guy.

But if all you know about James Squire is what you've read on labels on beer bottles, then you really don't know that much at all. This book – the first biography of Squire – separates the facts from the well-known myths. He never stowed away on the First Fleet ship carrying female convicts and didn't get lashed for stealing the ingredients to make beer.

He was also a man who may have used a false name on his daughter's birth certificate, loathed people who cut down trees on his property and got along far better with the natives than most of the other white newcomers.

Along the way you'll also discover a few other things about Sydney Cove, including Captain Arthur Phillip's efforts to get his hands on some Aboriginal heads for a friend, the early Australian fondness for cider rather than beer, the fight rival brewer John Boston had over a dead pig and the marine who tried to trade his hat for an Aboriginal child.

Friday Night at the Oxford

The story that led to reunion of legendary band Tumbleweed.
An in-depth look at Sunday Painters, a band decades ahead of
their time. Iconic shows like HOPE, HyFest and the Steel
City Sound exhibition. These are just of the more than 100
stories about Wollongong bands and events written by
journalist Glen Humphries for the *Illawarra Mercury*, from 1997
through to 2018, and his own short-lived website Dragster.
The 200-plus pages of *Friday Night at the Oxford* provide a
snapshot of what happened in the Wollongong music scene
over the last 20-odd years – the bands, the venues, the events.
It's a celebration of the music of a city.

So dig it.

Sounds Like an Ending

Midnight Oil, 10-1 and Red Sails in the Sunset

In 1982, Midnight Oil was a band in trouble. Their last album, *Place Without a Postcard*, was supposed to be their big breakthrough but it hadn't worked out that way. So they found themselves in London, feeling the pressure of recording what was a "make or break" album.

If this album went the same way as the last one, it could be the end of Midnight Oil. Out of the crisis came *10,9,8,7,6,5,4,3,2,1*, an album that changed everything for the band. It entered the charts and stayed there for more than three years. They started playing bigger venues - and they were able to pay back the bank manager.

Two years later, they headed to Japan to record the polarising *Red Sails in the Sunset*. It managed to do what *10-1* couldn't - give the band their first No1 album. But again the band found themselves facing the possibility it could all be over, courtesy of lead singer Peter Garrett's tilt at federal politics. If he wins, the band loses.

In *Sounds Like an Ending*, journalist and author Glen Humphries takes a track-by-track look at these two albums and the times and turmoil that fuelled them.

Night Terrors: The True Story of the Kingsgrove Slasher

Between 1956 and 1959, suburban Sydney was terrorised by a phantom known as the Kingsgrove Slasher. A peeping Tom, he graduated to breaking into houses to watch people sleep before later slashing women and girls with a razor while they lay in their beds.

He punched a 21-year-old woman into unconsciousness, breaking her teeth and cutting her mouth, hit a teenage girl in the face with a piece of wood and slashed a deep wound across the stomach of a 64-year-old woman. The Slasher also groped teens in their beds, and one of his 18 victims was just seven years old.

Night Terrors is the first detailed account of the Kingsgrove Slasher case. It draws on hundreds of newspaper articles written at the time - which show the level of fear in the community - as well as the transcripts from the court hearings, which had been sealed since 1959. The result is a true-crime book that might make it hard for you to go to sleep at night.

Biff
Rugby League's Infamous Fights

For close to a hundred years, the biff has been part and parcel of rugby league. And it was condoned for most of that time. As rough play like stiff arms, high tackles, spear tackles, facials and stomping were weeded out of the game, the punch remained. As recently as the 1980s league bosses would say there was nothing fans liked to see more than two forwards trading blows.

But the biff has all but disappeared in recent years, when the league finally realised there is nothing in the rule book that allows players to punch on. In Biff, Glen Humphries looks at some of the most infamous brawls in rugby league, from the Earl Park Riot and a match abandoned after it became a brawl to the most violent grand final and, finally, the punch that changed everything.

As well as offering a ringside view of the brawl, Biff also looks into the reasons behind the fights and what happened to the players afterwards. Some of them escaped suspension and some were rubbed out of the game, while others missed the chance to play in a grand final or found their careers cut short after being on the receiving end of a nasty punch.

Healer
The Rise, Fall and Return of Tumbleweed

With their long hair and fuzzed-up guitars, Tumbleweed rose
out of the ashes of late-80s Indie band The Proton Energy
Pills. Just over a year after their 1990 birth, they'd recorded
with Mudhoney's Mark Arm, scored a support slot on
Nirvana's only Australian tour (just as the grunge wave hit)
and signed a US record deal.

The Wollongong band hit their peak of popularity in the wake
of the 1995 album *Galactaphonic*. And then proceeded to shoot
themselves in the foot. Guitarist Paul Hausmeister got the
sack, and then drummer Steve O'Brien left in protest.

From there the band went downhill, releasing albums that met
an increasingly uninterested public and playing shows in front
of a half-dozen people. So it was no surprise when they called
it quits in 2001.

With the acrimony that swirled around the members for years
afterwards, it was hard to ever see the band getting back
together. But in 2009 they managed to heal their wounds and
reunite, releasing their fifth studio album a few years later and
survive the sudden death of bassplayer Jay Curley.

Journalist and music writer Glen Humphries has interviewed
the members of Tumbleweed numerous times and, in Healer,
takes the first complete look at the band's career.

EBOOKS

The Six-Pack
Stories from the World of Beer

From stories of monks making beer, to rumours of an unpleasant secret "ingredient" in a world-famous drink, there are plenty of great stories about beer. And six of them are captured in this ebook.

Beer is Fun!

Oh look, it's the best moments from Beer is Your Friend, the blog that won a national beer writing award and also inspired Dale to leave a comment "give ur self an uppercut u oxygen thief".

Why should you buy this book? Because it's 300-plus and it'll cost you just $2. What else in life will give you loads of entertainment for just $2? Go on, buy it. If you don't like it, I'll give you your money back. Well, that's a lie, I won't give you a cent, because I plan on holidaying in The Bahamas with the $2 you give me.